The Affiliate Start up guide!

Fast action strategies to start your affiliate marketing career!

Charlie Evans

Copyright © Charlie Evans, 2020

All rights reserved. No part of this book may be reproduced in any form on by an electronic or mechanical means, including information storage and retrieval systems, without permission in writing from the publisher, except by a reviewer who may quote brief passages in a review.

Table of Contents

Introduction to Affiliate Marketing 5

Setting Up Campaigns 13

Promoting Your Campaigns 21

Campaigns. The next step: Take action! 29

About the Author 31

Introduction to Affiliate Marketing

One of the most lucrative aspects of affiliate marketing is in being able to build an online income even without a product of your own.

While information development is an incredibly profitable market, when you're just entering the world of online business, affiliate marketing simplifies the process, while giving you the opportunity to gain hands-on experience without having to deal with the multiple tasks and responsibilities associated with being the developer or merchant.

For example, as an information product developer, you're responsible for all customer support enquiries and requests, and you need to spend time updating your product, working on keeping it consistently fresh and current based on market demand.

It's your job to satisfy customers, to handle refund requests, and to consistently work to optimise conversion rates.

As an affiliate marketer, however, you never have to spend any time on the product development, delivery or support issues, and instead, can focus on developing profitable campaigns that jack in commission payments 24 hours a day!

Your only job is to develop highly targeted campaigns that promote high quality products and then build powerful traffic campaigns that funnel in red-hot prospects who are interested in purchasing the products you promote.

Then, cash your commission cheques and rinse and repeat the process!

Affiliate marketing is not only incredibly simple to get involved in but it's a very rewarding experience.

It gives you the freedom to choose as many different niche markets as you wish, exploring countless opportunities and learning the ropes as you go. What other way can you "earn as you learn"?

So, now that you know just a few of the reasons why so many new marketers begin their journey into online business as affiliate marketers, let's take a closer look at what you can do to join the ranks of successful earners!

Choosing Products To Promote

Choosing quality products is an important part of every affiliate campaign, because you want to make sure that you are setting up campaigns around products that are likely to convert.

This means that you need to spend time carefully researching and evaluating products in order to create your "affiliate swipe file".

When it comes to choosing a niche, there are two methods that will help you get started:

1) Choose a niche that is evergreen
2) Identify demand and profitability based on existing competition

Take down notes of possible products and niche markets that look interesting to you.

Then, search for related forums, groups and blogs to determine what people are looking for, how big the market is and what is currently in demand.

Then, investigate keywords to determine how much competition is in the marketplace as well as how many searches take place each month for specific keyword phrases relating to each niche market.

If you plan to promote digital products, the best place to start looking for quality products is through ClickBank, available at http://www.Clickbank.com

ClickBank is the largest online marketplace for digital products, and you'll be able to quickly pinpoint hot sellers by browsing through their many categories.

ClickBank.com offers detailed statistics and information regarding each specific product making it even easier to quickly evaluate the profitability of potential campaigns.

Here is what these mean:

$/sale: The amount of money you earn for each sale.
Future $: Average rebill revenue.
Total $/sale: Average total $ per sale, including all rebills.
%/sale: The percentage of the product sale price that the sale represents.
%/refd: Fraction of publisher's total sales that are referred by affiliates.
grav: The measure of how many affiliates are promoting the product.

For each affiliate paid in the last 8 weeks Clickbank adds an amount between 0.1 and 1.0 to the total. The more recent the last referral, the higher the value added.

The Gravity indicator will tell you how well a product is selling. So a gravity score of 100 means a product is potentially selling better than one with a gravity score of 20.

When it comes to gravity assigned to any specific product, a gravity of 70 or higher is usually a good sign that the product is still in demand, and being actively promoted by other affiliates.

To take things a bit further, you can use free services such as www.CBTrends.com or www.CBEngine.com to further evaluate each product, in terms of performance, demand, and the number of affiliate marketer's that are promoting it (which is always a good indication of how profitable the market is).

There are many other affiliate networks and marketplaces worth exploring, with many offering a combination of both digital and physical products.

Here are a few to help you get started:

Amazon Marketplace

I suggest using Amazon to locate products primarily with a higher price point, as their payout rate is set at only 4%. Personally, I use Amazon only for products priced at $200 or higher to make up the difference in the low-end commission offer.

Still, the Amazon marketplace is a great way to monetise extra space on your website or blog, and with their extended affiliate options, such as being able to integrate an "astore" into your website, you're given a lot of flexibility as to how you can develop affiliate campaigns.

Tip: You can monetise your feeder sites with Amazon modules and plugins, just by logging into your Amazon Associates account and exploring their 'extended' options.

Commission Junction

Otherwise known as "CJ.com", Commission Junction has been around for many years and is known to pay on time and provide unbeatable support.

They also feature hundreds of merchants across the board spanning thousands of niche markets.

You may require approval prior to being able to participate in select affiliate programmes, as Commission Junction provides merchants the opportunity to pre-approve affiliates, but the application is extremely simple and you can expect to receive a response in a matter of a few hours.

Share A Sale

ShareASale.com has grown into an extensive affiliate marketplace, and since all merchants are required to retain a cash balance of funds used to pay affiliates, it's a risk-free way to ensure that you are paid for all of your efforts.

Pay Dot Com

PayDotCom is similar to ClickBank in that it only features digital products. One of the key differences between PayDotCom and Clickbank however is that when promoting products through PayDotCom, it's up the merchant to pay you, and this is done primarily through Paypal.

With ClickBank, you are paid by the company itself based on their payment schedule (every two weeks for paper cheque or weekly via direct bank transfer).

Setting Up Campaigns

The majority of your time as an affiliate marketer will be spent setting up campaigns. Campaigns involve a series of tasks, including developing squeeze pages, landing pages and most importantly - content pages.

Content pages offer information to visitors who land on the website, and essentially warm them up by giving them valuable information and then focusing that information about specific products.

For example, if you decided to promote a golf equipment package via Amazon's marketplace, you could create a content site based around golf.

You would offer a variety of resources including articles and resources that provided visitors with sufficient information about the niche, while promoting the golf package within the content.

Not only are content pages important in order to convert visitors into customers by providing valuable information, but they are important to your search engine ranking as well. Search engines will see that your website provides a lot of great content and is targeted towards relevant keywords, and in turn, will rank your website accordingly.

This means you'll be able to generate very high quality, organic traffic to your affiliate based content sites in a very short amount of time - and without paying a dime for traffic!

Here are a few ways to set up highly targeted affiliate campaigns:

Niche Based Websites

With niche-based websites, you simply select 10-20 products all based around a specific niche market. For example, weight loss or parenting.

You then construct an article-powered niche website that features 10 different articles, and at the bottom of every article, you feature a direct link to the merchant's website.

Niche based websites are very easy to set up, but just keep in mind that each website needs a specific theme. You want to segment your affiliate campaigns so that every website is focused around one specific market (or niche), so that you can funnel targeted traffic to your websites without convoluting the process.

Think about your websites structure from your visitors' perspective. If you were interested in finding out more information about the golf market, and you landed on a content website that had multiple categories where golf wasn't the main focus, not only would you likely exit the site but you wouldn't think it was an authority site.

Authority sites ALWAYS focus on one specific market segment, so that they can deliver quality and informative content that warms up visitors and maximises profits.

When creating your content site, hire a writer to create 10-15 keyword rich articles around different areas within that market.

For example, if you were to create an affiliate based content site on weight loss, you could create articles on all different aspects of losing weight, from healthy eating guides to work out routines.

Then, match up each article with a relevant affiliate product, and feature an ad box in the middle and end of each article, or integrate text based affiliate links within the content itself.

Product Specific Blogs

One of the easiest ways to create an affiliate based content website is to use the power of Wix blogs. With wix, you can get a free plugin of their powerful blogging software and have a fully functional, dynamic website created in under a few minutes.

Then, you can easily optimise your blog for the search engines using Wix's built in optimisation tools to customise your descriptions, key words and URL tag to get the best SEO results.

Blogs always rank quickly within the major search engines based on their SILO structure. A SILO is a targeted websites that is broken down into segments or individual categories.

Then, keywords are used to clearly describe each area of the site. Since SILO's help search engine crawlers explore the website, and identify the relevancy of your website based on the keywords featured throughout the site, blogs tend to rank quickly AND rank higher!

This can easily be done with Wix by simply creating different categories and assigning your blogs into the category they best fit into.

When creating affiliate content pages either with HTML or with blogs, make sure to choose a keyword-rich domain name that clearly defines what your site is about.

This will not only help search engines identify your website, but it will help human visitors instantly recognise your site based on included keywords. Plus, if you plan on promoting your website with PPC marketing campaigns, a direct, keyword rich domain name will increase your click through rates.

For example, if you are setting up an affiliate website focusing on weight loss, consider domain names such as:

WeightLossReviews
WeightLossIdeas
LosingWeightQuickly
HowToLoseWeight
WeightLossHub

When you upgrade Wix You get a free domain but if you use a different software you can register a domain name through www.GoDaddy.com

Review Websites And Pages

One of the easiest ways to create powerful, high performance affiliate websites is to use the power of a strong review.

Review based affiliate sites capture the sale as people looking for last minute information or reassurance regarding a product are always on the lookout for feedback and testimonials from customers who have purchased and used the product.

When creating your review website, you want to again, focus it on one specific topic.

Don't create a multi-level review site that spreads out its information or coverage across multiple niche markets, because you want potential customers to put faith in your review, and it's difficult to do that if you are writing dozens of reviews on various products in the same market, and giving each one a "thumbs up"!

People will only be motivated to purchase a product after reading your review, if they believe it is honest and thorough. People want to know that you'voe done your homework, or that you have personal experience with the products you are reviewing on your website.

This means you need to include both pros and cons about each product, highlighting the products strengths, but being upfront about any weaknesses in the product.

If you do this, your reviews will appear more genuine, and you'll find it easier to motivate visitors into taking action and closing the sale.

You may get a lot of search engine traffic for specific product names and model numbers. This is where review sites shine. Instead of trying to rank for a competitive phrase like "cell phones", you can instead rank for "brand name model number review".

So, make sure to optimise every review page to include the product title, authors name and other relevant keywords that will help visitors find your page within the search engines.

Promoting Your Campaigns

Once you have an affiliate content website ready for your market, it's time to begin driving targeted traffic to it!

You can do this a number of different ways, and in this segment of the report, we'll explore the most cost effective strategies to jump-starting your campaigns.

Article Marketing

One of the easiest ways of launching an affiliate campaign is by using article marketing directories.

With article content, you can simply submit it into the larger article directories and within minutes of being approved, can begin to see traffic flowing to your landing pages.

In exchange for providing them with free content, you get to include some text and links in a section at the bottom of each article called a resource box.

EzineArticles.com (http://www.ezinearticles.com) is the

biggest, most popular, highest-traffic article directory. They have tremendous authority in Google, and articles often rank extremely well, so they can get a lot of traffic.

As long as your articles are structured so that you are providing solid, useful content with a link back to your website showcased within the resource box, article marketing is a simple and effective strategy to generating prime traffic.

Another important thing to keep in mind is that you should always use anchor text within your resource boxes, rather than a direct link to your site. Anchor text will help you rank for many different keywords rather than just your website URL itself.

Here is the HTML code to use in your resource box if you want to use anchor text rather than a direct URL:

<a href=http://www.yourdomain.com" > Your Anchor Keyword Here </a>

You would replace yourdomain.com with your domain URL and include a relevant keyword phrase in the anchor text.

Your author's resource box needs to be as strong as your article's headline and contain information that will pull a reader in and motivate them to click on your link and visit your website.

Essentially, a resource box is very much like a fast-track commercial. You have only a few seconds to motivate them to read further and explore your website.

Here are the top five article marketing directories that I personally use for all of my campaigns:

www.EzineArticles.com
www.GoArticles.com
www.ArticlesBase.com
www.ArticleCity.com
www.ArticleDashboard.com

You can always choose to save time by hiring an Article submission service to automatically submit your articles for you.

One popular resource is available at:
http://www.SubmitYourArticle.com

Ezine Advertising

Advertising in newsletters can be a cost effective and very powerful method of spreading your affiliate links throughout the market very quickly.

When purchasing ezine (or newsletter) advertising, you always want to try to purchase "solo" ads, so that you are able to broadcast an article tied in with your affiliate link, without having to compete with other advertisers.

Here is a partial list of ezines that offer solo advertisement spacing:
http://soloadsonly.com/
http://www.bizopzine.com/
http://probiztips.com/
http://www.rent-a-list.com/

When contacting newsletter owners to promote within their broadcasts, you want to find out how many subscribers they have, as well as how many times they'll run your ad.

You also want a good idaea as to their overall open rate, and whether there are specific days where they've seen a higher response level.

To find more ezines to advertise in or to find ezines that are targeted towards non-IM niches, consider the following directories:

http://www.directoryofezines.com/
http://www.ezinelocater.com/
http://www.ezinehub.com

Feeder Sites

If you want to push your marketing message out to your niche market quickly, and absolutely free - you'll want to turn to feeder sites.

Feeder sites are free remotely hosted web services that allow you to create simple websites or web pages, such as Squidoo, available at http://www.Squidoo.com, who provides a free "hub building service" to anyone wishing to create a content rich web page.

Feeder sites are such a popular method of building targeted traffic campaigns because of how quickly they rank in the major search engines.

Since these websites are deemed "authority sites", they're already ranked high in engines like Google.com, and so by creating your sub-page on their server, your page will be discovered by search engine spiders, and ranked very quickly.

When creating your Squidoo lens, be sure to take advantage of the various modules that you can include on your page, and place a prominent link back to your main affiliate content page as well!

In addition, break up you content into short articles, and avoid linking to any related products until after the initial launch is over, since your focus is on funnelling this traffic through your affiliate link to the products order page.

For each feeder site, upload 1-2 keyword rich articles and spice up your pages with images, videos and use built in modules or plugins whenever possible.

When you've finished creating your feeder pages, ping each URL to get the traffic pumping in. You can do this with either http://www.Pingomatic.com or http://www.PingGoat.com

Here are the top feeder site resources to help you get started:

Blogger: http://www.Blogger.com
Wix: https://www.wix.com

WikiDot

This is a great way to get your sites ranking in the search engines quickly is by creating an account at http://www.Wikidot.com

Weebly

Create free websites and blogs, switch designs instantly, and features a drag and drop interface, Weebly helps you rank higher in search engines especially Google.
http://www.Weebly.com
http://www.WetPaint.com

Wet Paint features free wiki based websites that allow you to start your own social website instantly. Very good site for backlinks and ranking.

http://www.LiveJournal.com

Another free blog platform that will allow you to customise it from top to bottom including free themes and modules.

You now have the basics of creating profitable affiliate marketing.

Campaigns. The next step: Take action!

It all begins with choosing a single product and creating a quality content page that highlights the strengths and benefits of that product. Then, once you'voe been able to generate targeted traffic to your content page and you'voe seen results, begin working towards expanding your outreach by creating additional affiliate campaigns, focusing on new products and evergreen markets.

Affiliate marketing is an exciting industry to be a part of, and if you take consistent action in developing campaigns, creating high quality content and keeping a pulse on market trends and demand, you'll quickly reap the rewards.

I wish you the very best of success in your affiliate marketing career,
Remember to go to Add URL to take part the Super Affiliate Challenge and learn absolutely everything you need to know to replace your income within a ye**ar**!

About the Author

Charlie Evans is a Entrepreneur who specialises in website development, digital marketing and affiliate marketing. He is the founder of ECN Digital Development and the creator of The Super Affiliate Challenge.

After being homeless and managing to escape lifelong poverty Charlie know that he wanted to help others do the same. He believes that the best way to help someone is to give them the knowledge to help themselves, as the saying goes – " if you give a man a fish he will eat for a day but if you teach a man to fish he will eat for a lifetime".

To try and achieve this Charlie decided to start writing short books and creating online training to teach as many people as he could the techniques and strategies that helped change his life.

www.ingramcontent.com/pod-product-compliance
Lightning Source LLC
Chambersburg PA
CBHW030551220526
45463CB00007B/3064